EXPLAINING GRACE

The Divine Influence Upon The Heart

Pastors Cindi and Tim
we repect and love you
Both.
enjoy

EXPLAINING
GRACE

The Divine Influence Upon The Heart

BY GAYLE BRANNAN, JR.

Explaining Grace

The Divine Influence Upon The Heart

ISBN-10: 1544639015

ISBN-13: 978-1544639017

Printed in the United States of America.

Book Cover Design By: Daniel Jones, GoodBoy Records

Book Edited / Formatted By: Beverly Dobrich, Living Leaves LLC

Table of Contents

Foreword

In the contemporary Christian world, there are books that are written, sold and bought because of a catchy title or because the author is well-known and liked. This is one of the dangers in the current spiritual environment. I recently bought two books, both written by the same man of God, which I found I just could not read. The church needs books that do not just enhance the Ministry, but take the people of God forward in such a way that they are spurred to go beyond what they know, beyond what the pastor may be teaching and even beyond what the author of the latest book is writing. Too many books have provoked a passive form of Christianity.

We must also recognise that there is a plethora of books available within the Christian market that is based on the fundamental facet of grace. Yet this one is different because the style is not one that is set out to win either an adherent or an argument. This book, like any other that is written from the heart, must be read with an open mind, a willingness to obtain new understanding and the strength to be willing to change what has been believed for a long time.

I have known Pastor Gayle Brannan for many years, firstly as a worship leader and then as a church pastor, and I have met up with him every year since I began visiting the USA. I have seen him grow, I have also seen him emerge. It is refreshing to read the book of a man who is not copying what others have said and who sets out his own revelation and understanding in a way which is both clear and readable. Each paragraph is carefully crafted; there is a process of information that allows the reader opportunity to gain understanding and revelation. He may draw on what others have written: but the main thrust is that of a clear revelation that brings enlightenment (and therefore freedom) to all who love the Truth and wish to continue to learn.

This is the kind of book that provokes the believer to desire to go forward in knowledge. It is based on her revelation that is clearly going to increase and expand as the author grows in his intimacy with heaven, while his feet remain on the ground. It is not that there is a mingling or confusion of heaven and earth. It is much more about what is uniquely heard in heaven and is brought to earth with a simplicity and clarity that allows the reader (or, indeed, the hearer) to obtain revelation alongside understanding.

I would also describe this book as an accessible theological work. There is no need to hunt out words from the dictionary. The style is intimate, yet scholarly. For many, this book will open their eyes to a well-expressed presentation of grace, God and the believer, because it is written out of relationship with the Father.

Apostle Tony Howson (New Day International) Wrexham, UK

Truth is like an incredible, adventurous journey of discovery. It is like a divine treasure hunt. One of the greatest keys that I have discovered to this journey is seeing things through the eyes of covenant. There are several covenants throughout the Scriptures. Understanding which covenant is in operation will help you understand how God related to his people through the terms of each one of these covenants. Context, audience relevance, and the historic backdrop will turn the floodlight on that will expel much of the darkness. Sometimes truth will challenge some of your previous paradigms. If the result is a greater understanding of the manifold wisdom of God, and a deeper sense of relationship with Jesus, it is well worth the challenge.

In this treatise, Pastor Gayle helps us to focus on many difficult passages through the lens of the New Covenant. Seeing things through the lens of covenantal understanding will help one reconcile many of the hard questions in the Bible. Sadly, many Christians today have no idea that the New Covenant is not an addendum to the Old Covenant. It is a completely different covenant. For the most part, a lot of the church world today is a mixture of two covenants. The apostle Paul calls that a perversion of the gospel, because it is a mixture of law and grace. As you read the pages of this book, may I challenge you to allow the Holy Spirit, who is the teacher of the church, to cause the eyes of your understanding to be flooded with light. This book should not only teach you what you should think, it should teach you how to think for yourself as the Holy Spirit testifies to your spirit, what is truth and what is not.

This book will help you to move away from many of the toxic ideas that come from an orphan mentality; the flawed thinking that always has you begging for what you already possess through the finished work of Christ. It will bring you into an understanding that you are a son of God, and since you are a son, you are an heir of God and joint heir with Christ Jesus. It will cause you to have an abundant life as the divine supply of the grace of God satisfies your heart.

Dr. Lynn Hiles Th.D., Ph.D.
Lynn Hiles Ministries

In his introduction to the great Gospel bearing his name, The Apostle John makes a simple, yet profound statement about how God went about delivering His Grace to us. He said, "...the Law was given by Moses, but Grace and Truth came by Jesus Christ." Law is always impersonal. But Grace and Truth are always loving and personal.

In this book, Pastor Gayle Brannan goes about explaining, with great simplicity & compelling examples, what Grace is and how it works. Chapter after chapter unveils mountains of Truth about how a loving, thoughtful, & merciful Father has put a system in place where He shoulders the burden of our demerits and makes us right by the finished work of His Son, Jesus.

I challenge you to read this book with an open heart--as one seeking hidden treasure. You will find life! You will discover Truth. You will find answers to the questions you didn't know to ask. You will return to this book again.

Dr. Hart Ramsey
Senior Pastor and Founder,
Northview Christian Church

Introduction to *Explaining Grace*

By Bishop Ken Shelton
Shelton Covenant Ministries

When Pastor Gayle Brannan, my dear friend, asked me to write an introduction to his book on grace I, at first, thought that privilege should belong to the author. After all, there is a *Foreword* and several special comments from other leaders. However, after a short while, I came to see this as an opportunity to set the stage for many of the things that you will read in this book about grace.

Grace is a hot topic in the church world. Well-known preachers and teachers have landed on this gospel truth for good reason. Everything that has been accomplished to benefit others and to further the message of the Kingdom of God is because of grace.

You have, no doubt, listened to, read, and studied the topic of grace; unmerited favor. So what makes this book different? Why should you take the time to purchase and peruse yet another book about grace when there are so many? Well, I can answer that question for you.

Testimony:

Explaining Grace is more than a lexicon on a biblical subject; it is a glimpse at the revelation God used to rescue the author. I have known Gayle Brannan Jr. for roughly twenty years. When I first met him, he was a teenager with a divine gift to write, play and sing worship music from the heart. Later, as time moved on, I became acquainted with Pastor Gayle's heart for God. It is impossible to embrace the truth of God's grace without accessing our personal story and, yes, even failures.

We fail. There you have it. As human beings with flaws, we tend to aim too high, shoot too low, make too many promises, tell too many lies, and want too many things that are not ours. Tabloids and news channels spin the stories of the outlandish and unfortunate failings of famous people. An equal part of the human condition is our lust for these stories. Each day we hear about those who have broken the law, cheated on a spouse, created a Ponzi scheme or any of a thousand scandals. We know it will happen yet we shake our head in amazement.

Still others have been abused by someone they trusted causing a sense of shame. Sometimes they hide their story out of insecurity about what others will think of them. It is common for the victims of abuse to feel trapped even when they know they've done nothing wrong. Each instance is real and heartbreaking, but doesn't have to be the end of things. The greatest story of all isn't the grime of a person's shortcomings. It's not the grief of their victimization. Neither is it the grit of their self-determined comeback, but rather the grace of God that rescues us even when we cannot help ourselves.

Readability:

The mark of a gifted teacher is the ability to take great truths and present them with simplicity. That is what Jesus did. He spoke in parables. He told stories about fish, birds, lilies, wind and water to illustrate the meaning of His Kingdom. In a similar way, Gayle stays readable. He offers a timeless truth in a way that most anyone can grasp. He refuses to run down rabbit holes and chase incidental subjects but sticks to the story of God's grace, what it means, how it works, and what it does. That is the Gospel of Jesus!

This is possible because he has extracted these truths from his sermons. Each week, Pastor Gayle Brannan preaches to the congregation of Vertical Encounter Church in Detroit, Michigan. These are people that I know personally. I have heard these sermons and watched their impact on the lives of those who listen. I have come to know that Pastor Gayle really cares about people. The grace that changed him is the message that he preaches from his pulpit and that he presents to you here.

Challenge:

Pastor Gayle is not only a teacher and author, but he is also a student. He loves to read and to study the Word. He researches and double-checks his facts and information. The result is that even though his message is easy to understand, it is also challenging. As you read *Explaining Grace*, you may be challenged by an idea that he presents. That is the job of a writer presenting a familiar subject; it needs to bring something new or challenging with it. That is how you know it is not simply rehashed. Hirelings take responsibility for other people's revelation. A shepherd feeds the sheep with care and takes the responsibility seriously.

To be challenged means that the writer wants you to do your own research. When you prayerfully and open-mindedly research truths that are familiar, then the Holy Spirit is able to teach you. I John 2:27 (N.I.V.) reads, "*As for you, the anointing you received from him remains in you, and you do not need anyone to teach you. But as his anointing teaches you about all things and as that anointing is real, not counterfeit--just as it has taught you, remain in him.*"

It is the Holy Spirit who does the teaching. The writer presents the revelation that has been given to him. The conscientious reader takes that revelation and prayerfully researches the written word thereby making room for the Holy Spirit to plant His truth into your heart.

Inspiring:

We all love to be inspired. In fact, I love the etymology of that word. It is formed from two Latin word concepts: In and Spirit. We know that the Word of God is inspired (2 Timothy 3:16), but this message is also inspired. To be inspired means that you have been given a breath of truth. I believe that Pastor Gayle Brannan has prayed over this book. I also believe that God has breathed this message into Pastor Gayle. I hope that Explaining Grace inspires you from grace-to-grace (John 1:16). Or as the New International Version of the Bible reads, "Out of His fullness we have all received grace in place of grace already given." (NIV).

Chapter 1: Understanding A Covenant

Let me begin by saying that for years, I would read the Bible from the understanding that every word was present-day truth. I had no understanding of what the totality of the Canon was clearly saying. I would read things that seemed to contradict themselves, and because of my strict religious upbringing, I was taught to never challenge the Scriptures.

At that time in my life, I assumed God would have been offended if I questioned His book. After all, He had gone to such great lengths to preserve the original manuscripts for us all. Beware of my sarcasm.

I would read things like Psalm 51:11 (NIV), "Do not cast me from your presence or take your Holy Spirit from me," and then turn around and read Hebrews 13:5 (NASB), "*Make sure that* your character is free from the love of money, being content with what you have; for He Himself has said, 'I will never desert you, nor will I ever forsake you,' "

In my mind, I would think things like, “Why would David be begging God not to cast him away if God said He would never leave us.” Even though I just quoted Hebrews 13:5, the original passage that states that God will never leave us is found in Deuteronomy 31:6 (NIV) and it reads: “Be strong and courageous. Do not be afraid or terrified because of them, for the LORD your God goes with you; he will never leave you nor forsake you."

Some New Covenant teachers may say that because David lived before Christ, He would have had no understanding of a Father that never leaves us. The truth is that David, being a Jew, would have been intimately familiar with the Mosaic Law. The problem that David would have had was that the Law was only a shadow of things to come. Per Colossians 2:17 (NIV), “These are a shadow of the things that were to come; the reality, however, is found in Christ.”

Have you ever looked at the shadow of a person and appreciated the color of their eyes? Shadows reveal shapes, not character or characteristics. It was not until Christ that we saw the fullness of God’s intentions.

My point is that under the Old Covenant they would have seen only small glimpses of God's character and intentions. The Old Covenant was a shadow; the New Covenant is the substance. The Hebrew word for covenant is "berith" meaning marriage, contract, agreement, allies, or testament. Understanding the difference between covenants will help us rightly divide the word of truth.

The Old Covenant was the shadow;
the New Covenant is the substance.

Let's deal with the point at which the Old Covenant was initiated (Exodus, chapters 20-24). In Exodus 24:3 (NASB), Israel responds after hearing the laws and commands. "Then Moses came and recounted to the people all the words of the Lord and all the ordinances; and all the people answered with one voice and said, 'All the words which the Lord has spoken we will do!' "

Notice they said they would do all that the Lord had spoken. It is imperative to understand that they did not just say that they would do the Ten Commandments. In total, 613 laws were given to the people, and they agreed to obey them all. In other words, they made a covenant.

The purpose of the law (Romans 8:1-4, MSG):

> 8: 1-2 With the arrival of Jesus, the Messiah, that fateful dilemma is resolved. Those who enter into Christ's being-here-for-us no longer have to live under a continuous, low-lying black cloud. A new power is in operation. The Spirit of life in Christ, like a strong wind, has magnificently cleared the air, freeing you from a fated lifetime of brutal tyranny at the hands of sin and death.
>
> 3-4 God went for the jugular when he sent his own Son. He didn't deal with the problem as something remote and unimportant. In his Son, Jesus, he personally took on the human condition, entered the disordered mess of

> struggling humanity in order to set it right once and for all. The law code, weakened as it always was by fractured human nature, could never have done that.

The Law always ended up being used as a band-aid on sin instead of a deep healing of it. And now what the Law Code asked for, but we couldn't deliver, is accomplished as we, instead of redoubling our own efforts, simply embrace what the Spirit is doing in us.

You see, the purpose of the Law was to reveal sin. Paul the apostle says in Romans 3:20 (NIV), "Therefore no one will be declared righteous in God's sight by the works of the Law; rather, through the Law we become conscious of our sin.

Sin entered the world through Adam, but was not fully seen until the introduction of the Law.

Paul also says in 2 Corinthians 3:7 (NIV), "Now if the ministry that brought death, which was engraved in letters on stone, came with glory, so that the Israelites could not look steadily at the face of Moses because of its glory, transitory though it was,"

Did you catch that? The letters engraved on stone were the Ten Commandments. Paul is saying their purpose was death. The purpose of the Law was to show us that we cannot be righteous by our own efforts. The standard was so high that only God could do it.

When Jesus said, "Come to me all who are weary and heavy laden," He was talking about those who were worn out from the weight of the Mosaic System. Jesus was offering them REST by living through *His* obedience. I will deal with this more deeply later on.

Under the Old Covenant, our righteousness was as filthy rags; under the New Covenant, we are as righteous as Christ. We must understand the difference between Moses and Christ, old and new, shadow and substance, and life and death.

We have a better covenant with better promises as illustrated in Hebrews 8:6 (NLT): "But now Jesus, our High Priest, has been given a ministry that is far superior to the old priesthood, for he is the one who mediates for us a far better covenant with God, based on better promises."

This New Covenant we have is based on the obedience of Christ. We are who He has made us to be. Jesus did not just die *for* me, but AS me.

Chapter 2: Satisfied

Desperation is the language of the orphanage, while satisfaction is the language of the living room. Jeff Turner

My wife and I are now pastoring Vertical Encounter Church in Detroit, Michigan. Before we started pastoring, I had been doing worship for many years. I have been privileged to meet leaders from several different streams. The stream I was serving in would dictate the kind of songs I would lead. Some ministries were what I call WARFARE driven, and some would be more into the quiet, really wordy songs, while others like to shout the entire time. I have experienced them all. Let me say that I have no issue with any particular style of worship.

In 2007, I found myself in a difficult place in my life. It was a time of deep confusion accompanied by severe dissatisfaction. I would get home from Sunday morning church and just feel dead inside. I could not seem to understand where these feelings were coming from. I was starting to feel like I was doing religious circles and I wanted out.

There had to be more to God than what I was experiencing.

It was in the year 2009 that I finally started getting real answers. I remember driving home from a road trip in Ohio and still feeling frustrated with the circus that religion can become if not led by the Spirit, and the Spirit reminded me of a passage in the Gospel of John 4:13-15 (NASB):

> 13 Jesus answered and said to her, "Everyone
> who drinks of this water will thirst again; 14 but
> whoever drinks of the water that I will give him
> shall never thirst; but the water that I will give
> him will become in him a well of water
> springing up to eternal life." 15 The woman said
> to Him, "Sir, give me this water, so I will not be
> thirsty nor come all the way here to draw."

As I began to repeat this passage in my head, the Spirit brought my attention to verse 14, “but whoever drinks of the water that I will give him shall NEVER THIRST;” (Emphasis added).

It was like a brick just hit me in the face. “Wait a minute," I said to myself. "All of my favorite worship songs are about me being thirsty for God. Is it possible that my issue isn't a thirst thing, but more of a lack of awareness of what I already have in Christ?”

That moment began the journey in me that has changed my life forever.

In my travels during ministry, I have encountered sincere people who will say to me that they have had some powerful encounters with God while singing songs about being desperate or thirsty, or even being hungry. My response is always the same:

Joshua 10:12-13 (ISV):

12 Later that day, Joshua spoke to the Lord while the Lord was delivering the Amorites to the Israelis. This is what he said in the presence of Israel:

"Sun, be still over Gibeon!
Moon, stand in place in the Aijalon Valley!"

13 So the sun remained still
and the moon stood in place
until the nation settled their score with their enemies.

This is recorded, is it not, in the book of Jashar?

The sun stood in place
in the middle of the sky
and seemed not to be in a hurry
to set for nearly an entire day.

It is important to understand a couple of things here. Joshua lived in a time where there was no understanding of our solar system. He would not have known that the sun NEVER moves. He was asking God to give him more time by keeping the sun in the sky so that there was enough light to finish the battle. In other words, Joshua prayed a sincere prayer with ignorance. I have found that we can be sincerely wrong.

The reason it gets dark at night has nothing to do with the sun rising or falling; it has everything to do with the earth rotating. The truth is that God bypassed Joshua's ignorant request, and stopped the turning of the earth.

Many people make the mistake of attributing the blessings of God to their right-believing rather than to God's just being good. After all, it is the goodness of God that leads us to repentance. Repentance in the Greek language is the word "metanoia" (met-an'-oy-ah) meaning a change of mind, change in the inner man. Goodness comes first and causes us to change our minds.

Many people make the mistake of attributing the blessings of God to their right-believing rather than to God's just being good.

I want to give you just a few scriptures to help you see that satisfaction was always the goal of our father.

According to Matthew 5:6 (NLT), "Blessed are those who hunger and thirst for righteousness, for they will be filled." Look at the end result here; it does not say that those who hunger and thirst will remain hungry and thirsty. Hunger comes from lack.

Colossians 2:10 (NIV) says, "and in Christ you have been brought to fullness. He is the head over every power and authority." As you can see, we have the fullness of Christ *now*. You cannot get a double portion of full. Sorry, I couldn't resist! Most of our problems in life flow from our hunger.

Satisfied

I love watching animal shows and recently, while watching a documentary about lions, one man said something profound. He said that a lion's work hours last only as long as he's hungry; once he's satisfied, the predator and prey live peacefully together.

I believe satisfaction is the key to relational harmony in our lives. Psalm 90:14 (NASB) says, “O satisfy us in the morning with Your lovingkindness, That we may sing for joy and be glad all our days.”

David had a prophetic picture of Christ while saying this. Our true morning does not come from the sun, but rather, the SON. Christ Jesus is our new day, our Sabbath, our green pasture and our resting place.

If I needed a hundred dollars and you gave it to me, wouldn't my need be satisfied? Of course! What would be your response if I was still begging you for a hundred dollars? You would most likely direct my attention to what you have already *given*. This is how many of us worship. Our songs say, “God, I am thirsty or hungry or desperate,” and we never stop to think about how that makes Jesus feel. He has *given* us all things, yet we are still begging for what we already possess.

The truth is that those of us who are in Christ do not need another drink, but rather, an awareness of what we have drunk. If we could only start worshipping from the foundation of satisfaction, we would become more aware of the open heaven that resides in us.

Chapter 3: New Heaven and New Earth

As we begin chapter 3, I cannot help but think of how many times I used to read the teachings of Jesus and just feel confused. So many times, I would come away wondering how I could ever live up to the standards that Jesus has set.

For instance, in Matthew 18:8-9 (MSG), it says: [8] "If your hand or your foot gets in the way of God, chop it off and throw it away. You're better off maimed or lame and alive than the proud owners of two hands and two feet, godless in a furnace of eternal fire. [9] And if your eye distracts you from God, pull it out and throw it away. You're better off one-eyed and alive than exercising your twenty-twenty vision from inside the fire of hell."

Let's really think about that for a second. Verse 9 (NIV) says, [9] "And if your eye causes you to stumble, gouge it out..."

The truth is if we really took everything that we read seriously, we would all be blind at some point. There is no one alive that at some point hasn't looked at something or someone with ill intentions. And it was this type of teaching that used to really bother me as I pursued a deeper relationship with the Lord. I knew in my heart that I could never truly live up to that sort of standard. And this is just one of several passages that teach the perfection of the Law.

When I started to rightly divide the Word of Truth and understand the difference between the Old Covenant and the New Covenant, I began to have peace and clarity.

When I started to rightly divide the word of Truth and understand the difference between the Old Covenant and the New Covenant, I began to have peace and clarity.

Sadly, many Christians still do not understand the magnitude of what Christ has done for us at the Cross.

One of the scriptures that I want to begin with is Romans10:4 (ESV). "For Christ is the end of the law for righteousness to everyonc who believes."

Did you catch that? Christ is the end of the Law. We must understand that Christ fulfilled the requirements of the Law for us. Romans 3:22 (ESV) declares, "the righteousness of God through faith in Jesus Christ for all who believe."

This is hard for some Christians to understand. As a pastor who travels and teaches in several different arenas, I get all kinds of questions. One of the most common questions that I get among Christians concerns Matthew 5:17-18 (NIV). It says, 17 "Do not think that I came to destroy the Law or the Prophets. I didn't come to destroy them, but to fulfill them, 18 because I tell all of you with certainty that until heaven and earth disappear, not one letter or one stroke of a letter will disappear from the Law until everything has been accomplished."

Before I give some apologetics concerning this passage, let me start by saying context is key. Ben Witherington, a known theologian whom I hold in high regard says, and I quote, "A text without a context is just a pretext for whatever you want it to mean." We must study the Bible in light of its original historical, archaeological, literal theological and ethical context.

In Matthew 5:17, we need to understand what is truly taking place. First, we need to understand what the "new heavens and new earth" really mean in this passage.

In 2nd Peter 3:11-13 (NASB) it says, [11.]"Since all these things are to be destroyed in this way, what sort of people ought you to be in holy conduct and godliness,.[12.]looking for and hastening the coming of the day of God, because of which.the heavens will be destroyed by burning, and the elements will melt with intense heat! [13]But according to His promise we are looking for new heavens and a new earth, in which righteousness dwells."

Some critical things are going on here that we need to pay attention to. The first is that the heavens will be destroyed by burning and the elements will melt with intense heat. Please notice that the heavens and the elements must be in the same place. The elements are simply the tools or furniture that were used in the temple where Levitical sacrifices were offered. This passage in Peter is talking about the destruction of the Temple which we know happened in the year 70 AD.

The temple was everything to the Jew. It is where they offered up animal sacrifices for the forgiveness of sins. To have had this taken away from them must have been devastating.

A good point of reference to understand the importance of the temple for the Jewish people is in 1st Kings 8:43 (ISV), "then hear in heaven where you reside, and do whatever the foreigner asks of you, so that all the people of the earth may know your name, fear you as do your people Israel, and so they may know that this temple that I have built is called by your name."

The question that should arise when reading this passage is, "How are the heavens being burned?" It's simple, really. In this passage, we are not talking about the heavens as some place in the sky, but rather, a physical place in the earth. To be even clearer, it's specifically talking about the temple.

I have already referenced that to get a clear understanding of context, we must research history as well. A well-known historian who lived in the first century wrote and testified concerning Jesus in the context of first century history. This is a quote from Josephus concerning the destruction of the temple and how the Jews perceived the temple.

“However, this proportion of the measures of the tabernacle proved to be an imitation of the system of the world:” *(Antiquities,* Book 3, Chapter 6, Paragraph 4, Section 123).

The Jerusalem Temple had been built to look like a microcosm of the universe. We typically overlook how literally true the Temple Hymn preserved in Psalm 78:69 (ESV) is: "He built his sanctuary like the high heavens, like the earth, which he has founded forever."

Another critical point in 2nd Peter 3:13 is to understand the Greek word used here for *new*. There are two words used for new in the New Testament. Those words are "neos" and "kainos". Neos means new in time; something that has never been before. Kainos means new in quality or nature, or superior in value or better than the old. Peter was using the word kainos here. If Peter meant that God was going to physically destroy the heavens and the earth and create a replacement, he would have used the word neos.

So the truth is that in Matthew 5, Jesus was talking about replacing an old system with a new system. He was talking about the destruction of the physical temple that the Jews viewed as Heaven and Earth. Remember, Jesus ended verse 18 with the statement "...until everything has been accomplished."

Three words that Jesus spoke changed our lives forever, "It is finished!" Jesus was declaring that all is accomplished. The death, burial and resurrection of Jesus were both the destruction of an old system and the birthing of a new system.

You and I have always been the ultimate destination of the Father. We are *The Dwelling Place*. Even in the Old Testament when Moses was constructing the temple that was beautiful inside and filled with gold and expensive furniture, God said to cover it with bloody badger skins.

Exodus 26:14 (NIV) says, “Make for the tent a covering of ram skins dyed red, and over that a covering of the other durable leather.” Even in the Old Testament, the temple where God dwells was still covered with skin.

This was a type and shadow of what was to come. I love what Paul the Apostle told the Corinthian Church in 1st Corinthians 3:16 (NIV): “Don't you know that you yourselves are God's temple and that God's Spirit dwells in your midst?”

You and I are the representation of a New Covenant which is to say a new agreement between Heaven and Earth. After all, we *are* called the body of Christ.

Chapter 4: Receiving Grace

Most of us have heard the definition of grace at least one time in our life. For those of you who do not know, it comes from the Greek word “khar'ece” which simply means acceptable, favorable or unmerited favor. However, my favorite definition for Grace is: *The Divine influence upon the heart*.

Sometimes we can know something in our head that we do not experience in our heart. For years, I understood in my head that Grace meant unmerited favor. The problem was that I was still working for right standing with the Father.

When I first started studying the Grace of God, it was very difficult for me to understand. I was raised in deep legalism and dogmatic teachings. Although it was never said exactly this way, the environment I was raised in suggested that if you did not believe like we did, then you were wrong. Many of you can identify with that.

My upbringing had several different components to it. To this day, my mother is a born-again believer who loves God with all of her heart. She tried her best with what she had to bring us up in the ways of God. However, my father was an alcoholic, and did not have the best reputation in the city or within our family. As a young boy, I have vivid memories of watching my dad get drunk and then act disorderly; sometimes even becoming violent.

My father and my mother divorced before I was ten. Even though my mom made the best decision she could at that time in her life and did what was right, it still left a deep void on the inside of me. For years and years, all I wanted was a relationship with my dad. It did not seem to matter to me what condition he was in at the time. As I got older, I began to resent him for not being there. It festered into unforgiveness, and I became very angry with him.

By the time I turned 23 years old, I had taken a ministry position in Flint, Michigan. In my heart, I had moved past the idea that I would ever have a relationship with my father. Then one night, at 4 o'clock in the morning, I remember being awakened from a dream that showed me prophetically that my father was sick and also gave me details as to his location.

God was asking me to drive 2 hours from where I lived at 4 o'clock in the morning to go pick up a man that never really wanted anything to do with me! You can only imagine what I was going through emotionally at that moment.

To make a long story short, I was obedient. I drove to Battle Creek, Michigan, to pick up my father who was lying on the floor, bleeding internally. As I approached him, the Holy Spirit spoke to him through me and said that if he would pack up and leave with me right then, and leave his old life behind, God would do a miracle in his life. I am proud to say that he did just that, and God blessed him tremendously in the months to come.

Backing up just a little bit, here, I want you to understand how I felt driving this stranger of a father back to my house to live with me. In my heart, I did not want to help him. I harbored deep and severe unforgiveness. The fact that God wanted to redeem this man's situation was, honestly, offensive to me. My heart was asking God, “Why can't you use somebody that this man has not hurt to bring reconciliation to him?” Needless to say, this was the beginning of my journey of understanding Grace.

I began to learn very quickly that Grace will offend our flesh. It was in this season of my life that I began to realize just how legalistic I truly was.

God was setting me up. God was getting ready to use my dad to teach me the heart of the Father. It's actually kind of funny, now, that God would use my father to teach me the greatest lesson I've ever learned in my life.

I am so grateful that God taught me how to forgive my father, because in the seasons to come, I would need that same Grace for myself. God knew what he was doing.

One of the devastating things about legalism is that it keeps us blind to our own condition. Have you ever heard the saying, ”Get your act together”? Well, if you do get your act together, you're still just acting. That is exactly what the Law does. It never takes healing to the root of the issue. Grace gets down into the deepest part of who we are and heals us from the inside out. Life truly begins the moment we can embrace our true identity as sons and daughters and live from the freedom that Jesus gave us.

I have learned that before we can really, truly understand the Grace of God, we must experience it.

In Luke 7:47 (NIV), we read, "Therefore, I tell you, her many sins have been forgiven—as her great love has shown. But whoever has been forgiven little loves little."

In other words, those who have been forgiven much, love much. I find that the most radical worshippers and disciples of Christ are those who have been rescued from the deepest, darkest places. People who have been forgiven much are those who do not need a worship leader to lead them to a place of worship. They are their own worship leader. After all, the Bible does tell us to let the redeemed of the Lord say so.

I want to present you with a couple of examples of how God prepares our hearts for receiving Grace.

Law:

Many people do not understand the purpose of the law. One of the problems that we have in church today is not that people are preaching cheap Grace, but that they are preaching cheap law. If people truly understood how impossible it is to live up to the standard of the Law, they would have wanted Grace from the start.

In 2nd Corinthians 3:7-8 (NIV), Paul says, [7] "Now if the ministry that brought death, which was engraved in letters on stone, came with glory, so that the Israelites could not look steadily at the face of Moses because of its glory, transitory though it was, [8] will not the ministry of the Spirit be even more glorious?"

Did you catch that? Paul is calling the Ten Commandments the ministry that brought death. Essentially, he is saying that the purpose of the Law is to reveal our sin nature. It is meant to wear us out. He was not saying that the Law was bad; he was saying that the Law set a standard too high to reach.

Matthew 11:28-30 (NIV) says, [28] "Come to me, all you who are weary and burdened, and I will give you rest. [29] Take my yoke upon you and learn from me, for I am gentle and humble in heart, and you will find rest for your souls. [30] For my yoke is easy and my burden is light."

When He said, "all of you who are weary and burdened," Jesus is addressing people that are worn out from trying to fulfill the Law and all of its regulations. You see, the Law would produce death IN US, while Jesus produces life. Many people do not understand that the purpose of the Law was to wear us out so that we would be ready to receive the Grace that only Jesus can give to us.

In Matthew 5:3 (NIV), Jesus says, "Blessed are the poor in spirit, for theirs is the kingdom of heaven." It's imperative to understand the Greek definition of the word *poor* here, which is "ptochos," meaning to crouch. See, Jesus was talking to people who were under the weight of the Law and saying blessed are you who have been trying to bear this weight. Then he finishes it with "...theirs is the kingdom of heaven." Notice that Jesus is removing the weight of the Law and giving them the Kingdom.

The point I'm trying to make here is that God will use the Law to wear us out so that we will accept the Grace that He offers.

Failure:

The second thing that God will use to position us to receive Grace is our failures. Some people only learn what God is trying to get them to learn when they are in a season of failure. Self-righteousness and pride typically walk hand-in-hand. I want to show you some things in Scripture that helped a man by the name of Peter come into the ultimate revelation of Grace.

In Matthew 18:21 (NIV) it says, "Then Peter came to Jesus and asked, 'Lord, how many times shall I forgive my brother or sister who sins against me? Up to seven times?' "

First of all, I find it funny that Peter is the one asking this question. He is the most offensive guy on the team. Wow! The guy that causes the most problems in the group is the one asking how many times he should forgive somebody else. But let's bypass that for a moment.

It is important to understand that Peter was a Jew, and there are certain disciplines that Jewish people have. In that day and age, Jews would recite Old Testament Scriptures everyday with their families. Peter would have been intimately familiar with the Book of Amos.

Amos 2:1-2 (ISV) says, [1] "This is what the LORD says: 'For three transgressions of Moab because they cremated the bones of the king of Edom, burning them to lime. [2] So I will send fire upon Moab, and it will devour the fortified citadels of Kerioth. Moab will die in the uproar of battle, with a war cry and with a trumpeting of the Ram's Horn.' "

In other words, God judged Moab because he sinned three times. Can you imagine only being able to sin three times before God judges you? We would not even be able to get through an hour of our day without the Judgment of God raining down on us.

It is highly possible that Peter had this old paradigm in his head while asking Jesus how many times he should forgive his brother who sins against him.

When Jesus answered Peter's question in Matthew 18:22 (NIV), [22] “Jesus answered, ‘I tell you, not seven times, but seventy-seven times.’ ” Jesus was introducing a completely different paradigm to Peter. This was a new revelation that Peter had never heard of, never even considered.

It's not that easy to embrace a new way of thinking when for so long, you've been thinking a completely different way. After all, the word repentance simply means a change of mind.

The thing that I love about Jesus is that he never demands Peter to change his way of thinking instantaneously. Isn't it amazing that there's even Grace for that!

In the Book of Luke, we see how Jesus responds to Peter bragging about his faithfulness. Luke 22:33-34 (NIV) says,
33 "But he replied, 'Lord, I am ready to go with you to prison and to death.' "

34 "Jesus answered, 'I tell you, Peter, before the rooster crows today, you will deny three times that you know me.' "

Did you catch that? Peter would deny Jesus three times. Remember Peter's old way of thinking was three strikes, you're out! Jesus always knew that one day Peter would need Grace after having sinned three times.

The truth is that God will use a season of failure to position us to receive the greatest revelation of Grace that we've ever known. The Law forces us to believe something, but Grace invites us to experience His love. The more that I've grown in Grace, the more thankful I am that love is patient.

Before I end this chapter, let me just say to you that Grace is a person. It is Jesus Christ, and He loves you unconditionally. He died to make us righteous. Learn to put faith in what He has died to give us.

Chapter 5: Jesus The Exact Representation

"Jesus is perfect theology." Bill Johnson

In the last chapter, I made a statement saying that Grace is a person. In this chapter, we will talk about Jesus who is Grace embodied. Jesus is the lens through which we view the Father. Many Christians have a view of Jesus that is not biblical. In this chapter, we are going to discuss the purpose and mandate that was on the life of Jesus.

Hebrews 1:1-3 (NIV) says, [1] "In the past God spoke to our ancestors through the prophets at many times and in various ways, [2] but in these last days he has spoken to us by his Son, whom he appointed heir of all things, and through whom also he made the universe. [3] The Son is the radiance of God's glory and the exact representation of his being, sustaining all things by his powerful word. After he had provided purification for sins, he sat down at the right hand of the Majesty in heaven."

I want to shed light on verse 3 which says that the Son is the radiance of God's glory and the EXACT representation of His being. I have read this scripture almost my entire life and never really comprehended that Jesus is the exact representation of the Father.

I have read this scripture almost my entire life and never really comprehended that Jesus is the exact representation of the Father.

In other words, everything that we see in Jesus is 100% the father's intention. We cannot say that about any other biblical figure. As one man has said, Jesus is perfect theology. Theology by definition is the study of God, and in order for us to understand God, we must start with a model that is flawless. As much as I love David and Paul, Jeremiah and Isaiah, and Ezekiel and all of the other biblical figures, none of them fully represented the intention of the Father.

As a matter of fact, the question I had to ask myself was if the entire Bible is 100% accurate according to the will of God, then why would you need to send a flawless copy?
By the way, God is not offended by our questions.

One of the functions of the Christ was to teach humanity the heart of the Father. All throughout the Old Testament, there are several occasions where biblical figures such as Moses, Isaiah, Elijah, David and several others misrepresented the heart of the Father. I am going to give you a few examples, before we dig deeper into the Mandate of Christ.

Numbers 20:5-11 (NIV):

> 5 "Why did you bring us up out of Egypt to this terrible place? It has no grain or figs, grapevines or pomegranates. And there is no water to drink!"
>
> 6 Moses and Aaron went from the assembly to the entrance to the tent of meeting and fell facedown, and the glory of the Lord appeared

> to them. [7] The Lord said to Moses, [8] "Take the
> staff, and you and your brother Aaron gather
> the assembly together. Speak to that rock
> before their eyes and it will pour out its
> water. You will bring water out of the rock for
> the community so they and their livestock can
> drink."
>
> [9] So Moses took the staff from the Lord's
> presence, just as he commanded him. [10] He
> and Aaron gathered the assembly together in
> front of the rock and Moses said to them,
> "Listen, you rebels, must we bring you water
> out of this rock?" [11] Then Moses raised his arm
> and struck the rock twice with his staff.
> Water gushed out, and the community and
> their livestock drank.

What is happening here is that the Hebrew people are now complaining, because they are stuck in the wilderness without the provisions that are necessary for them to live. They have all too soon forgotten what God just did for them by bringing them out of Egypt. Isn't that something? God doesn't take us from miracle to miracle, but rather, from miracles to faith or from answers to questions or from promises back to processes.

Moses was the leader of these people and at this point, found himself becoming irritated with their complaining. Remember, now, the Bible says in Numbers12:3 that Moses was a very humble man; more humble than anyone else on the face of the Earth. The majority of scholars believe that it was Moses who penned the first five books of the Old Testament also known as the Torah or the Pentateuch.

This is just a side note, but if Moses wrote that he was the most humble man on the face of the Earth, wouldn't that contradict his own humility?

Either way, he was just a man, and none of us are perfect. We must remember that during this time, Moses was the mediator between the Father and the people. Their relationship with and understanding of God depended completely upon Moses. What Moses said and did concerning God would paint their perception of the Father. In verse 7, Moses went before God and brought up the need of his people. God responded and told Moses to speak to the rock. It should have been very clear that the command of God was to speak to the rock. However, in verse 11 we see that Moses went before the people and struck the rock. To some people reading it nowadays, it may not seem as if it was too big a deal. After all, they did get to drink water. The problem is that even though they were experiencing a miracle, it wasn't what the Father told Moses to do.

We have to understand that throughout the Old Testament, the Father was trying to reveal His nature to His people. The Father's intention was twofold: 1) God wanted to meet their physical need, and 2) God wanted His people to understand His true nature. If we continue reading, we see that God rebukes Moses and Aaron because they were disobedient to what He said.

That may seem harsh to us, but, as I have said, we must understand that Moses was the mediator between the people and God. It's not just about what Moses did, but rather, *how* Moses did it. He had distorted the nature of the Father. Even though these people had water to drink, in the back of their minds they were probably still thinking that God was mad at them. The truth is that God is not mad at us and has always been gracious and slow to anger.

There are far too many Christians today that are sitting under leaders that are not reflecting the True Heart of the Father. They look nothing like Jesus. No wonder people have a distorted idea of who God really is.

Under the Old Covenant, the Bible is filled with people who misrepresented the heart of the Father or, you could say, the Kingdom of God. We must understand that the Kingdom is simply a country where God's heart is put on demonstration. As a matter of fact, the renewed mind puts on a demonstration of the realities of His country.

In Matthew 11:12-13 (NIV), it says, [12] “From the days of John the Baptist until now, the kingdom of heaven has been subjected to violence, [13] and violent people have been raiding it."

You see that the kingdom of God has been taught or high jacked by violent men. Just like we see some leaders today that don't portray the heart of the Father accurately, we also saw it back then.

As a matter of fact, if you read the Book of Jonah, you will find out that the reason Jonah was avoiding Nineveh was because he knew that God was going to be graceful to them. The history between the Ninevites and the Hebrews was hostile. In other words, God was sending Jonah to his enemies to reveal the goodness of the Father.

It would probably have been much easier for Jonah to go to Nineveh with a message of doom and gloom rather than repentance. See, God was showing the Ninevites that He was merciful, but showing Jonah that He loves all humanity, not just the Jews. In essence, God was saying, "Your enemies are not my enemies."

Maybe this is why Jesus said, “Love your enemies,” but never said, “Love my enemies.” God has always been trying to send the message that He loves us with an everlasting love, and that He's gracious toward us.

This brings us to Jesus, the perfect representation of the Father. In John 14:9 (NIV), [9] “Jesus answered: ‘Don’t you know me, Philip, even after I have been among you such a long time? Anyone who has seen me has seen the Father. How can you say, ‘Show us the Father’?”

Jesus is boldly declaring that if you have seen him, then you have seen the Father. Wow! What a statement. Finally, somebody who represents the intention of the Father flawlessly. Not only does he do the Miracles, but also does them with the right nature. Finally, we get to see what our heavenly Father is really like.

One of the tragedies during the time of Jesus was that the Church did not recognize him as the son of God, but would claim to know God. See the nature of God had been so distorted that they did not even recognize Jesus, the exact representation, when He came.

Jesus was showing those who followed him the true intention of the Kingdom. He would eat with sinners, heal the sick, love the unlovable and forgive the most severe offenders.

In his book, *The Prodigal God,* which I highly recommend, Timothy Keller talks about the parable of the father and his two sons, more commonly known as 'The Prodigal Son' story.

In his book, he begins to elaborate about three conditions that are based on the context of Luke 15:1-2: 1) the older brother represents the Pharisees; 2) the younger brother represents the tax collectors and sinners; and 3) the father represents our heavenly Father.

As I began to read this book, the most beautiful revelation came to me. Jesus did not feel the need to go into this story until the religious people arrived. In other words, it wasn't the tax collectors and sinners that were missing what He was teaching; it was the religious people who were still under the distorted teaching of their predecessors.

This story's purpose was to show the religious people how the Father truly responds to both the younger brother syndrome and the older brother syndrome. Jesus teaches that the father is being invited into both of their conditions and both of their failures.

The true purpose of Christ was to redeem humanity and correct the distorted image of our heavenly Father. Anything that does not look like Jesus is not God.

When reading the Gospels, let's let the nature of Jesus teach us of the nature of God. And as we grow in the nature of God, let's begin to demonstrate to the world who the Father really is.

The Holy Spirit has a major role to play in this process. In the next chapter, we will be discussing the importance of the Spirit.

Chapter 6: Forgiveness and Freedom

"Many people hate the Law because it opposes their freedom, but do not love Christ enough to manage it."
Gayle Brannan

In the last 10 years, I have seen several teachers and preachers start transitioning to the Gospel of Grace. And although I am extremely grateful to see this transition, one of the things that has become dangerous is the imbalance that is taught concerning Grace.

I will be the first to say that when I started coming into the revelation of Grace, I taught it with an imbalance. I am grateful to have a church that understands their leader is growing just as they are growing. I have since corrected some of the doctrine that I was teaching so that our congregation would benefit from the balance of thorough doctrine.

Before we get too far into this chapter, let me just say that when I use the term balance, I am not talking about 50% Law and 50% Grace. John 1:17 (NIV) says, “For the law was given through Moses; grace and truth came through Jesus Christ.”

First of all, let's notice that truth is on the side of Grace here, not Law. In other words, Grace reveals truth to us and IN US.

One of the mistakes that I made when teaching Grace in my earlier years was that I would simply focus on just being forgiven and covered by Grace. Many people will use that revelation to live a lifestyle that does not reflect the heart of Christ. And although we are completely covered and forgiven, we must not stop there. When grace has its perfect work in us, per Titus 2:12 (NIV), “It teaches us to say ‘No’ to ungodliness...”

And although we are completely covered and forgiven, we must not stop there.

I have a lot of friends who teach Grace and New Covenant principles that have phenomenal insight. I'm surrounded by critical thinkers who, at a scholarly level, dedicate themselves to understanding truth. And although I value some of their insight, I've begun to recognize that many of the friends that I dialogue with at that level are not pastors and have never pastored people.

You may be wondering what pastoring has to do with it. The truth is that pastoring affords us the opportunity to both teach people and then, to see how the teaching affects their personal lives.

I've learned that in order to be most effective in people's lives, we need to preach the entire truth. The most deceptive lies ever told still carry a portion of the truth. The Apostle Paul was the premier voice concerning Grace teaching in the

New Testament. When studying his teachings, you will find the balance of Grace, freedom and life in the Spirit.

I want to discuss two major components of Grace:

1) We are forgiven.

Understanding that we are completely forgiven is critical to the New Covenant believer. When I was younger and under legalism, I would constantly ask God, every single day, sometimes four or five times a day, to forgive me for my sins.

I specifically remember a time when I was very young and was at church with my mother, and the pastor of the church said that God was going to rapture us that night. Wow! I could not believe what I had just heard. Needless to say, I did not sleep that night. I was up the entire night asking God to forgive me for the last thought I just had. I was terrified.

What if I had a bad thought right before Jesus came? As funny as that may sound to some of you, at that moment, to me, it was very real. I did not understand at that age that I was completely forgiven in Christ.

Colossians 2:13 (CEV): “You were dead, because you were sinful and were not God’s people. But God let Christ make you alive, when he forgave all our sins.”

Isn't it amazing that he has forgiven all our sins? Some people think that God is only forgiving the sins that we can confess, but this is not true. The truth is that on the Cross, Jesus dealt completely with the sin issue.

Jesus actually dealt with the sin of the world. It's amazing to me how many people missed what really happened at the cross. Jesus was not just forgiving people who would make him Lord and Savior but also the world. John 1:29 (NIV): “The next day John saw Jesus coming toward him and said, “Look, the Lamb of God, who takes away the sin of the world!”

We treat God as if he is sitting in heaven holding a grudge against us until we apologize. Wouldn't that contradict the very teachings of Jesus when He taught us to forgive our enemies? Matthew 5:44 (NASB) says, “But I say to you, love your enemies and pray for those who persecute you.” It wouldn't make sense for Jesus to tell us to forgive our enemies if He could not do it Himself. The truth is that Jesus is the most radical demonstration of forgiveness.

In Luke 23:34 (BBE, 1965) we read, “And Jesus said, Father, let them have forgiveness, for they have no knowledge of what they are doing. And they made division of his clothing among them by the decision of chance.”

Notice that it does not say “Father, forgive them for they know not what they have DONE”; instead, it uses the word DOING. Did you catch that? Jesus is asking God to forgive them while they are still in the process of killing him. It is easier to forgive people who have stopped hurting us, but far more difficult to forgive somebody who is still hurting us.

Let's look at 2 Peter 1:5-9 (NIV):

> 5 For this very reason, make every effort to add
> to your faith goodness; and to goodness,
> knowledge; 6 and to knowledge, self-
> control; and to self-control, perseverance; and
> to perseverance, godliness; 7 and to godliness,
> mutual affection; and to mutual affection,
> love. 8 For if you possess these qualities in
> increasing measure, they will keep you from
> being ineffective and unproductive in your
> knowledge of our Lord Jesus Christ. 9 But
> whoever does not have them is nearsighted
> and blind, forgetting that they have been
> cleansed from their past sins.

This passage changed my life forever. Peter is saying to add to your faith goodness, knowledge, self-control and godliness. In other words, you can still be in the faith while working out all of these things. The most revelatory thing about this passage is that in verse 9, Peter says that those who do not have these characteristics have forgotten they have been cleansed from their past sins. Did you catch that? Notice that Peter is using past tense here.

Do you see that at the Cross we have been completely forgiven past, present and future? Understanding that we are completely forgiven is the first step in changing our perception about ourselves. Condemnation breeds toxic thinking.

2) We have Freedom.

Freedom serves a critical role in changing us from the inside out. It is also freedom that scares many legalistic Christians. You have probably heard one or two people say that God has called you to higher standards. As I have already said, much of my upbringing was legalistic, so I have heard all of the quote, unquote holiness arguments.

In the years that I have preached the Gospel of Grace, I have been accused of giving people a license to sin. I'm sure most of you have heard the same thing if you are preaching Grace. Let me first say that if you are preaching the Gospel of Grace correctly, you should definitely get that response from some people.

In Romans 6:15 (NIV) it says, "What then? Should we sin because we are not under the law but under grace? By no means!" People love to quote this verse when trying to bring balance to the Gospel of Grace "in their minds". What I would like to point out is that when you read chapter 5, Paul makes such a strong argument for Grace that by the time he gets to chapter 6, he must address the issue.

Although it was never my intent, I recall the first time that I was accused of giving people a license to sin. I know better than most how sin can destroy your life in the most devastating ways. Over the years, as I have continued to grow in my understanding of Grace and the love of the Father, I began to really think this accusation through. When asked the same question today, my response is simple: YES.

This may be shocking for you to hear, but please hear me out before making me out to be what some would call a heretic. 1st John 1:8 (NIV) says, "If we claim to be without sin, we deceive ourselves and the truth is not in us." It is extremely important to understand that every Christian, no matter how much they pray or fast, has sin in their life in some measure. As a matter of fact, there would be no need for us to live by Grace if we had no sin that needed covering.

I, for one, thank God that I am covered by Grace knowing that when I do sin, He is there to cover me at all times. Romans 5:20 (KJV) says, "Where sin abounds Grace much more abounds." Giving people a license to sin is much different than endorsing a sinful life.

I absolutely agree that sin will rob you of all that is good in your life. It is very true that sin produces death. By no means is it my desire for anybody to embrace a lifestyle of sin. I want to see the fullness of God's plan come into fruition in everyone's life, and to do that, they must manage their freedom and follow the Spirit.

Freedom and our ability to choose are the only things that expose the true condition of our heart. If I was a drug addict and locked away in prison for three years, would it be fair for me to say that I am free from the addiction of drugs just because I have not had a taste in three years? The answer is no. I may have been sober for three years, but it is completely due to the fact that I have not had a choice to make.

The fact is that our maturity can only be measured when we have the freedom to make a choice. I believe one of the reasons why God put *that* tree in the garden was to give Adam a choice.

Without a choice, we would never know what really means the most to us. Many people want to paint the outside of the house and never deal with what's on the inside. Jesus described those having this condition as people who were whitewashed tombs. There are many people who never change, because they've been pretending to be whole for years. They have been taught how to speak, how to dress, how to preach and what disciplines to mimic. On the outside, they are programmed robots advertising religion at its best.

The Gospel was always meant to save us from the inside out. It affects the very core of who we are. It gives us true identity and teaches us to love all, the way the Father loves us. People do not change because we tell them to; they change because they're ready to. The more we encounter Jesus, our true identity, the more we rediscover who we really are. As we continue to grow in the Spirit, we will begin to manage our freedom with greater responsibility.

Acts 16:25-30 (NIV):

> 25 About midnight Paul and Silas were praying
> and singing hymns to God, and the other
> prisoners were listening to them. 26 Suddenly
> there was such a violent earthquake that the
> foundations of the prison were shaken. At once
> all the prison doors flew open, and everyone's
> chains came loose. 27 The jailer woke up, and
> when he saw the prison doors open, he drew
> his sword and was about to kill himself
> because he thought the prisoners had
> escaped. 28 But Paul shouted, "Don't harm
> yourself! We are all here!"

> 29 The jailer called for lights, rushed in and fell trembling before Paul and Silas.
> 30 He then brought them out and asked, "Sirs, what must I do to be saved?"

I love this passage of scripture when it comes to describing what responsible freedom looks like. Many people would rejoice in the fact that they were free from prison. Honestly, many of us would have left claiming it was the will of God. What I find fascinating here is that these men had a choice. They could have left the prison and served their own interests, or remained to demonstrate the heart of the Father.

Thankfully, they chose to remain. God presented them with freedom in the hope that they would deny themselves so that their jailer would see the heart of God.

Notice that while still in the prison, Paul and Silas were singing spiritual songs and hymns to the Lord. Their mind was focused on the Father even while in the dungeon.

What we go through is not as important as how we go through. I believe their ability to make the right choice with their freedom was determined by the mindset they entertained when imprisoned.

The choices we make will always be the result of the mindset being entertained. Whatever has our focus also has our future.

Chapter 7: The Spirit Life

We will never value a voice we do not understand. Gayle Brannan

To the Christian, the Holy Spirit is everything. We cannot function properly or live from purpose without Him. The renewing of our mind begins as we surrender to the leading of the Spirit, and then, once we are under Grace, we are free to grow in the Spirit.

When reading the New Testament, it is impossible not to see how important the Holy Spirit is in the life of the believer. Every miracle and moment of discernment that we read about was man surrendering to the wisdom of the Spirit. The Holy Spirit is the ultimate teacher.

John 16:13 (NIV) says, "But when he, the Spirit of truth, comes, he will guide you into all the truth. He will not speak on his own; he will speak only what he hears, and he will tell you what is yet to come."

I would like to point out a couple of things here. First of all, I would like to bring your attention to the beginning of verse 13 where it says that the Spirit of truth will guide you into all truth. It is amazing to me that truth is not just told to us, but we are guided into it. Truth is not something we just hear, but rather, something we experience.

WHO WE ARE can be revealed to us by the Father using WHERE WE ARE to see if we will trust His leading. I've learned that the Father can use any situation I go through to reveal to me his intention for my life.

The second point I want to bring to your attention is in verse 13 when it says He will not speak on His own; He will speak only what He hears. This is a critical point in understanding the Holy Spirit. Everything the Holy Spirit leads us to do is coming from the Father's intentions. He is revealing to us God's desire for our lives. I believe that one of the ways to understand the Holy Spirit is to study the life of Jesus. It is extremely easy to think we're hearing the Spirit when we are really not.

See, the Holy Spirit bears witness of Christ. The more we are in tune with the nature of Christ, the more we will understand the Holy Spirit's leading. The Holy Spirit will always look like the Father and the Son. The life of Jesus displayed the Spirit without measure. Jesus was the ultimate, mature son. The maturity of our sonship is only seen as we surrender to the Spirit.

When I first came into the revelation of Grace, like most people, I was merely focusing on the freedom that I have in Christ. It was a few years after having focused on that freedom that I began to realize the purpose of my freedom. The ultimate goal of freedom and forgiveness is to release us to a life in the Spirit. Without the Holy Spirit, we can do nothing that reflects the Father.

It is important to understand that while in the Old Testament, the Spirit was on us; in the New Covenant, the spirit is IN US.

1st Corinthians 3:16 (NLT) says, "Don't you realize that all of you together are the temple of God and the spirit of God Lives in You?"

You see, under the Old Covenant, the Spirit was given in portions, which is why Elijah could give Elisha a double portion. Under the New Covenant, we have been given the fullness of God. John 1:16 (NIV) "Out of his fullness we have all received grace in place of grace already given."

Over the years, I have heard it said that all of life's answers are found in the Bible. I would have to honestly disagree with that and say that all of life's answers are found in the Spirit. I am not trying to discredit the Bible in any way; it's just that in 2017, we are dealing with things that they never would have dealt with in biblical times.

One of my favorite quotes is, "We can never expect to do the miracles that were done by the apostles in the Book of Acts if we value a book they did not have over the Holy Spirit that they did have," by Bill Johnson. So, when we read about the mighty exploits that were done in the New Testament, we need to keep in mind that the only thing they were following was the leading of the Holy Spirit. Sure, there was some knowledge of the Torah, but there were several things the Holy Spirit told them to do that were in direct contradiction to the Torah.

Acts 10:9-16 (NASB):

> 9 On the next day, as they were on their way and approaching the city, Peter went up on the housetop about the sixth hour to pray. 10 But he became hungry and was desiring to eat; but while they were making preparations, he fell into a trance; 11 and he saw the sky opened up, and an object like a great sheet coming down, lowered by four corners to the ground, 12 and there were in it all *kinds of* four-footed animals and crawling creatures of the earth and birds of the air. 13 A voice came to him, "Get up, Peter, kill and eat!" 14 But Peter said, "By no means, Lord, for I have never eaten anything unholy and unclean." 15 Again a voice *came* to him a

> second time, "What God has cleansed, no *longer* consider unholy." [16] This happened three times, and immediately the object was taken up into the sky.

A couple things are going on here. Number one, Peter was a Jew who was raised with the lawful tradition of not eating any unclean animals. To the Jew, an unclean animal was an animal that was offered to false gods. Peter had been taught by the Law and Jewish custom that it is not right or holy to eat these animals. Please understand where Peter's perspective was coming from. It was from the knowledge of the Law recorded in the Old Testament.

He is now confronted with the Holy Spirit as he is on the rooftop experiencing a vision. The Holy Spirit is asking him to partake of unclean animals which is a direct contradiction to the knowledge that he has according to the Old Testament. Notice that the Holy Spirit is asking something new of Peter that was forbidden in the Old Testament.

Peter and the rest of the Apostles would soon realize the importance of listening to the Holy Spirit. Jesus was more interested in us living by the Spirit, than by the letter of the Law.

Another reason I bring this passage up is because some people will say the Holy Spirit will never contradict scripture. I would agree if they were talking about New Covenant passages.

However, it is clear that the Holy Spirit will ask us to do things differently than the way things were done under the Old Covenant. I am not suggesting that all of the Old Covenant has been thrown away. However, I am suggesting that there are parts of the Old Covenant such as the Levitical System that are fulfilled in Christ.

Our maturity is defined not in our scriptural knowledge, but in our ability to walk with the Spirit. It is the Spirit that gives us wisdom in all things.

Our maturity is defined not in our scriptural knowledge, but in our ability to walk with the Spirit. It is the Spirit that gives us wisdom in all things.

1Corinthians 2:8-10 (NASB):[8] *the wisdom* which none of the rulers of this age has understood; for if they had understood it they would not have crucified the Lord of glory; [9] but just as it is written,

> "THINGS WHICH EYE HAS NOT SEEN AND EAR HAS NOT HEARD,
> AND *which* HAVE NOT ENTERED THE HEART OF MAN,
> ALL THAT GOD HAS PREPARED FOR THOSE WHO LOVE HIM."

[10] For to us God revealed *them* through the Spirit; for the Spirit searches all things, even the depths of God.

Notice that in verse 9, Paul is quoting the Old Testament, Isaiah 64:4, but then he goes on to say that to us, God has revealed them through the Spirit. We must understand that the Spirit gives us a knowledge of God that those who had to rely on the Old Testament did not have.

Another passage I want to bring to your attention is in Galatians 5:22-26 (NIV) which reads, [22] "But the fruit of the Spirit is love, joy, peace, forbearance, kindness, goodness, faithfulness, [23] gentleness and self-control. Against such things there is no law. [24] Those who belong to Christ Jesus have crucified the flesh with its passions and desires. [25] Since we live by the Spirit, let us keep in step with the Spirit. [26] Let us not become conceited, provoking and envying each other."

I remember a time when I was trying to walk in love, joy, peace and all of the other attributes of the Spirit. I would constantly exhaust myself trying to mimic the Spirit life. I was approaching this passage in Galatians the same way that I would approach the Law of Moses. I would try, try, try. It became very much an impossible task.

When I was in my early 20s, I remember one night as I was praying about a relationship that was becoming irritating, I began to hear the voice of the Holy Spirit. I remember him asking me to forgive this individual. After an hour of wrestling with that concept, I finally began to surrender in my heart. I remember feeling kind of weird as I got up off of my floor in my little apartment. It was like the irritation had gone.

To my surprise, I started to realize how much I loved this individual. As a matter of fact, the moment I began to realize that I loved this individual was the moment I became more patient with this individual.

The revelation started to hit me that Galatians 5 is not about striving to become, but rather, trusting to become. After all, it is called the fruit of the Spirit. All of the attributes listed in Galatians 5 are the aftermath of having fellowship with the Spirit. You see, the Holy Spirit will love people through us. If we would spend more time praying for people and forgiving people than we do complaining about people, we would have an easier time dealing with people by the Spirit.

There is much more that I could say about the importance of the Spirit in this chapter as He is the most essential ingredient in our spiritual makeup. I will finish this chapter with the hope that you will begin to fellowship with the Spirit and allow Him to guide you into all truth knowing that your purpose and identity flow from Him and Him alone.

Remember, the purpose of freedom is to serve the mandate of the Spirit.

Chapter 8: What's Love Got To Do With It?

> **Children are God's gifts to parents so that we may understand unconditional love.** Gayle Brannan

As a young boy, my mother used to take me to church with her all the time. It seemed as if we were in church every night. I'm not really sure how she found out about all of those church services throughout the week. All I know is that I grew up going to church a lot.

My mother loved to go to revivals. Some of you may be reading this and not know what I'm talking about when I use the term "revivals". They don't hold them as frequently anymore, but when I was a boy, we used to go to revival services which could last anywhere from three nights in-a-row to seven consecutive days.

I remember just kind of going through the motions that were expected of me. At a young age, my mom would have me sing in church and play the drums when needed. I didn't really mind too much, because there was a girl that I was attracted to that would always be there, because her mother and mine were good friends.

As the years went by, I was burning out with doing Church. My family had gone through significant challenges which were causing me to resent God somewhat. And even though my heart was getting farther and farther away from church and what it represented, my mother would demand that my brothers and I attend services faithfully.

I remember being somewhere around 14 or 15 when my church hired a new youth pastor. I was a bit skeptical because of my prior relationships with youth pastors. I remember one night my mother told me to come in the house and put something nice on, because we were getting ready to go to church. What I did not know is that the church we were going to be attending that night was the church that my new youth pastor would be singing at.

Now, anybody that knows me knows that I love music. As we walked in the door, I remember thinking I hope this guy is cool, because my mother is going to make me spend a lot of time with him.

As we sat through the service, the first 30 to 40 minutes seemed to be status quo. Then came the moment when my future youth pastor walked on stage and grabbed his guitar. But as he adjusted his microphone and began to sing worship songs, I remember feeling multiple things. I thought to myself, "Wow, this guy can really sing!" Then I thought to myself, "I cannot wait to meet him and show him that I can sing, too." As I was sitting there listening to him sing, something started to come alive in me. I started to sense the presence of God like never before.

Needless to say, tears began to flow as God dealt with my heart. I remember trying to describe to a friend what that moment felt like. I told him that all I knew was that I am loved. It was in this moment that the trajectory of my life was changed forever.

It is absolutely impossible to encounter God without sensing His overwhelming love for you. I am so thankful for that moment in time because it has forever influenced my heart in the way I see God, myself, and all people.

The love of Christ is unconditional. It is like no love that we have ever experienced. He walks with us through the deepest valleys and comforts us in the darkest seasons.

The love of Christ is unconditional. It is like no love that we have ever experienced. He walks with us through the deepest valleys and comforts us in the darkest seasons.

Hebrews 13:5 (NASB) “I will never desert you, nor will I ever forsake you,” The more that I am convinced of His love for me, the more it frees me to love the world like He loves me.

LOVING GOD

I remember one day while studying about love, I came across a passage of scripture in Romans 8:28 (NIV) and it reads, [28]" And we know that in all things God works for the good of those who love him, who have been called according to his purpose."

As I was reading this passage, I thought to myself, "Wow! God works all things for the good of those who love Him, not to those He loves." This revelation messed me up, because I was always focusing on God's love for me. And although that is extremely important, it is critical to understand that when dealing with our purpose, it is important for us to also love God. Let me explain this passage with more detail.

In this verse, the word *loves* that is used is the Greek word "agape" meaning the highest form of love, charity; the love of God for man and man for God. It is unconditional love that transcends, that serves regardless of circumstances.

In other words, this scripture is telling me that I need to love God unconditionally, also. At first thought, you may think that it's easy to love God unconditionally, because He never does anything that would offend me. Believe me when I tell you that I thought the same thing. I learned very quickly that my unconditional love for God would be tested the moment He started pruning me. I also realized that it's easier to submit to correction that we agree with.

You see, loving unconditionally means that I have to trust His judgment even when I don't understand. One of the worst things that we can do is to prove that our love is not unconditional by leaning to our own understanding. Loving God unconditionally requires our faith; trusting what He sees that we cannot see.

LOVING PEOPLE

The goal of the Father is to love us so effectively that it becomes contagious and ignites our affections toward others. 1 John 4:19 (KJV) says, "We love him, because he first loved us."

In my study time, when researching a particular passage of scripture, I always read several interpretations of the

Scripture. As I began to go through the various translations that I have available to me, I began to realize that the majority of the translations read a little differently than the King James Version. For instance, 1st John 4:19 (NASB) reads, "We love, because He first loved us."

As I began to research why this is different, I found out that the word "him" used in this passage is actually omitted. It is not in the original Greek text here. You may be wondering why that matters? For me, it makes a big difference, because if you use the King James version which says we love HIM because He first loved us, some people will justify not loving other people.

I personally like the NASB much better, because once we realize that we are first loved by Him, we begin to love. Period. God is love and His desire is that we become love as well. There is no greater belief in the universe than believing you are loved. The creator of all things is deeply and affectionately in love with us.

John 13:35 (NIV), “By this everyone will know that you are my disciples, if you love one another.” The world recognizes Jesus, not by how many worship songs we sing in their presence, or how loud we pray, but simply, by how we love one another. If what we have with God is real, it will always reflect in the way we love each other.

One of my favorite passages in the Bible concerning love is found in 1st Corinthians 13:4-8 (NIV). It reads, [4] “Love is patient, love is kind. It does not envy, it does not boast, it is not proud. [5] It does not dishonor others, it is not self-seeking, it is not easily angered, it keeps no record of wrongs. [6] Love does not delight in evil but rejoices with the truth. [7] It always protects, always trusts, always hopes, always perseveres.

[8] ‘Love never fails. But where there are prophecies, they will cease; where there are tongues, they will be stilled; where there is knowledge, it will pass away.”

There are days when each of us has a difficult time loving someone else. If we're being honest, all of us get irritated with someone from time-to-time. It is on those days that I try to remind myself of this passage of scripture.

As I was reading it one day, I began to realize all of these attributes of love are responses to some sort of drama. What's even more critical to understand is that this passage of scripture strips us of our fleshly rights. I don't know about you, but when I'm irritated with somebody, the last thing I'm trying to hear is that love is patient. Thank God that He never gives up on us. For any relationship to be successful, these qualities must be practiced and experienced.

Loving people the way God loves them will produce more change in them than the Law could ever do. In the times in which we live, what the church needs is a Love Revolution. After all, love never fails.

Chapter 9: Fallen From Grace?

Christianity is less about us holding onto God and more about God holding onto us. Gayle Brannan

Over the years, I have heard the term "fallen from Grace" several times with many implications attached to it. When I first heard the term, it was always in the context of someone sinning or failing in their moral responsibility as a Christian.

When I first heard the term, it was always in the context of someone sinning or failing in their moral responsibility as a Christian.

I remember sitting, listening to certain people talk about other people and thinking to myself, "What are we going to do now to help them?" It was like the only thing people wanted to do was just to talk about each other. Restoration did not seem to be of any importance in the conversations I was a part of.

I remember a certain season in my life when I just could not seem to whip my flesh into submission, and the harder I tried, the worse it had gotten. All that I knew about God was primarily from the influences that I had in my life at that time. Needless to say, I was under the impression that I had fallen from Grace. In my mind, I had reached a place that Grace could not rescue me from. It was almost as if I was going to have to climb out of the hole that I, myself, had dug.

I am extremely proud to say that, today, I can testify that not only does His Grace work completely, but the arms of Jesus reach much further than our failures. I love the scripture in Romans 5:20 (KJV) that says, “But where sin abounded, grace did much more abound:”

The term “fallen from Grace” comes from the Book of Galatians, chapter 5. When we read this passage in context, it will explain clearly what Paul meant when using this term.

Galatians 5:1-5 (NIV):

> 1 It is for freedom that Christ has set us
> free. Stand firm, then, and do not let
> yourselves be burdened again by a yoke of
> slavery.
>
> 2 Mark my words! I, Paul, tell you that if you let
> yourselves be circumcised, Christ will be of no
> value to you at all. 3 Again I declare to every
> man who lets himself be circumcised that he is
> obligated to obey the whole law. 4 You who are
> trying to be justified by the law have been
> alienated from Christ; you have fallen away
> from grace. 5 For through the Spirit we eagerly
> await by faith the righteousness for which we
> hope.

Allow me to give you some history concerning the book of Galatians. The entire Book of Galatians is Paul's effort to correct the heresy of the Judaizers who were trying to tell people that they had to be circumcised and follow the Jewish Law to be saved.

In Galatians 4:4-5, Paul explains at length that we are not saved by Law or rituals. In chapter 5, he is talking about circumcision. That if a person trusts in circumcision to save them, then Christ is of no value.

Paul was Furious! He even went so far as to say that he wished the people who were trying to convince the Galatian believers to be circumcised, would emasculate themselves. If you don't know what emasculate means, let's just say that as a man, you'll never use the restroom the same way again. Paul was literally saying, "Don't stop with circumcision; remove it entirely!"

According to Paul, falling from Grace is US putting our faith in the Mosaic Law. In other words, we are working for righteousness rather than trusting for it.

Who were the Judaizers?

Let's start by looking at the church of Galatia. Paul started several churches in the province of Galatia and then moved on to other regions. While Paul was away edifying and building other churches, he began to hear that other people and teachers had gone into the church of Galatia and began to teach people that Jesus is good, but that they needed to also obey the Law of Moses.

In other words, these Judaizers were undermining the Gospel of Grace and the finished work of the Cross. They were a group of Jewish Christians in the first century CE (500-1500) who preached to the recently founded Gentile churches and tried to conform them to the Law of Moses even after the death and resurrection of Christ.

We also see them in Acts 15:1-2 (CEV) which reads, [1] "Some people came from Judea and started teaching the Lord's followers that they could not be saved, unless they were circumcised as Moses had taught. [2] This caused trouble, and Paul and Barnabas argued with them about this teaching. So it was decided to send Paul and Barnabas and a few others to Jerusalem to discuss this problem with the apostles and the church leaders."

Even here, we see that both Paul the Apostle and Barnabas are arguing with the Judaizers. It is really quite simple; the Judaizers were on a mission to mix Law and Grace within the church.

While some people may think that Judaism was only influential in biblical days, I hope to enlighten you. There is a growing movement in the earth today that is teaching that the Mosaic Law is still in effect. Not only does this undermine the work of the Cross; this is witchcraft according to Paul.

After all, in Galatians 3:1-2 (ESV) he says, [1] "O foolish Galatians! Who has bewitched you? It was before your eyes that Jesus Christ was publicly portrayed as crucified. [2] Let me ask you only this: Did you receive the Spirit by works of the Law or by hearing with faith?"

I find it funny that the Apostle Paul, being a Jew who at one point took the Mosaic Law extremely literally, is now an advocate for Grace. Paul would defend the doctrine of Grace with extreme passion. The zeal he once used to endorse the law, he would now use to preach Grace. If there was anyone who understood the purpose and intention of the Law, it would have been Paul.

You see, the mixture of Grace and Law is deadly. It neutralizes both Grace and Law, and makes the cure for sin ineffective. It's similar to taking two different medicines, one for high blood pressure and the other for low blood pressure, at the same time. The two will counteract each other, and the patient will not receive the benefit of either. He could die as a result of trying to cure himself by taking both medicines simultaneously.

Let's look at Ephesians 2:8-9 (NIV):

> 8 For it is by grace you have been saved, through faith—and this is not from yourselves, it is the gift of God—
> 9 not by works, so that no one can boast.

See, even here, the Apostle Paul is teaching the doctrine of Grace to the church at Ephesus. Notice that Paul says it is a gift from God. Under Law, everything we get, we have to earn; everything is a free gift under Grace.

The truth is that if Grace cannot be earned, it can also not be taken away. However, it is possible that your faith in Grace can be taken away. If we listen to a mixture of Law and Grace, it will affect our faith in Grace and the finished work of the Cross. We must continue to meditate about the finished work of Christ.

You must remember that the true fight that we are engaged in is the fight of faith or the fight of belief. 1st Timothy 6:12. "Fight the good fight of the faith. Take hold of the eternal life to which you were called when you made your good confession in the presence of many witnesses."

I want to leave you with 2nd Corinthians 5:20-21(GNT):

> 20 Here we are, then, speaking for Christ, as
> though God himself were making his appeal

through us. We plead on Christ's behalf: let
God change you from enemies into his friends!
[21] Christ was without sin, but for our sake God
made him share our sin in order that in union
with him we might share the righteousness of
God.

WOULD YOU LIKE GAYLE BRANNAN TO SPEAK AT YOUR CHURCH OR EVENT?

Booking

Email him at:

gaylebrannanjr@comcast.net

Available on iTunes

or email to order:

gaylebrannanjr@comcast.net

61822288R00075

Made in the USA
Lexington, KY
21 March 2017